Exploring
Galápagos

Written by Kerrie Shanahan

Illustrated by Derek Schneider

Flying Start
to Literacy®

Contents

Preface   4

A long voyage   6

Going ashore   8

A surprising find   14

Proof!   18

Back on the *Beagle*   28

Epilogue   30

A note from the author   32

Preface

In 1831, an English sailing ship called the *HMS Beagle* embarked upon a five-year voyage of discovery around the world. One of the places the ship visited was the remote and isolated Galápagos Islands. These islands straddle the Equator in the Pacific Ocean and are over 800 kilometres off the west coast of South America.

The Galápagos Islands are situated far enough away from other landmasses that the native wildlife is very isolated from the rest of the world. As a result, many of the animals on these islands are unique, with unusual characteristics not seen anywhere else in the world.

Galápagos Islands

On board the *HMS Beagle* was the scientist Charles Darwin. Darwin studied the diverse and rare wildlife he encountered on the Galápagos Islands. He collected specimens, created realistic drawings and made notes about the wildlife he observed.

Also on board the ship was a servant cabin boy named Syms Covington, who was only 16 when the *HMS Beagle* set sail on its five-year voyage. By the time the ship arrived at the Galápagos Islands, the-19-year old was working as Charles Darwin's personal servant. Syms was fascinated by what he saw on the islands.

This is a fictional diary about the adventures that Syms might have had, as he explored the incredible Galápagos Islands with his mentor, Charles Darwin, over 180 years ago.

A long voyage

September 10th, 1835

I have been on the ship now for almost four years. *Four years!* It feels like forever since I saw Mother and Father. I do miss them but I would not swap what I have done for the world.

As I reflect upon my time as a servant boy on the ship, I acknowledge that there have been good and bad moments. At times, it certainly has not been fun – cleaning lavatories, scrubbing floors and running errands for short-tempered officers. But, at other times it has been a once-in-a-lifetime opportunity. I've seen places all around the world that I could only dream about.

The last two years have been the highlight of my journey so far. By an excellent stroke of luck, I was promoted to be Mr Charles Darwin's personal servant. He is a scientist who studies nature – animals and plants. His ideas are

fascinating. When I was a little boy, Mother would always find me collecting bugs and slugs and all sorts of critters in the small patch of land at the end of our street. It is little wonder that I enjoy helping Mr Darwin with his work.

One day I would like to study nature like Mr Darwin does. But I have not been to university like he has. Luckily, I did go to school long enough to learn to read and write, so I am capable of becoming his assistant. Such a position is my hope and dream. For now, I am only Mr Darwin's servant and I must not get ahead of myself.

Going ashore

September 16th, 1835

Today, we got our first glimpse of one of the
Galápagos Islands. There are 16 islands in
the group and we are going to be exploring
some of them over the next month or so.
Little is known about these islands and what
might be found on them. Mr Darwin is very
excited about what he might see. I have heard
that the land is arid and hot, and that the animals
living there are unusual.

I could not believe my luck when Mr Darwin
informed me that I would be joining him and
going ashore. He said he needed me to help with
the collection and documentation of plant and
animal specimens. This is my chance to impress
Mr Darwin. I very much want to become his assistant.

We are presently anchored in the Pacific Ocean, just off the coast of one of the islands. Tomorrow, we will board a small boat and go onto the island. Maybe if I work very hard, Mr Darwin will notice what an asset I am to him and that I am knowledgeable. We will see!

September 17th, 1835

Today we set foot on the first of the Galápagos Islands.
These islands were formed millions of years ago by
erupting volcanoes. The ground was rocky and black
from the hardened volcanic lava. And, it was hot. Not
simply hot like a summer's day. It was hot as if we were
enveloped in the heat of a fiery furnace. Mr Darwin said
the heat radiated off the black rocks making it feel even
hotter than it actually was. And I believe him!

We saw huge tortoises on the island. Giant ones. They were so enormous that I could have ridden on their backs! Mr Darwin said he had heard about these creatures but to see them with his own eyes was exciting. They moved very slowly and showed no sign of fear when they saw us. We observed them graze on grasses and eat cactuses.
I made some sketches of the tortoises and Mr Darwin told me that they were realistic. I tried to hide my pleasure when I received this praise, but I could not. I smiled. I felt very proud.

We also collected several different plant species. I volunteered to make a record of these once we returned to the ship. It will be arduous work, but it is another way for me to impress Mr Darwin.

Towards the end of our day of exploration on the island, a strange thing happened. As we were walking back to the shore to return to the *Beagle*, I saw a most unusual sight. Out of the corner of my eye, I saw a lizard scramble across the rocky shore and dive into the water.

At least I thought that is what I saw. I know enough about animals, however, to know lizards are not sea creatures, and surely they don't swim. So, maybe I was mistaken.

I was uncertain about whether I should mention these lizards to Mr Darwin or not. On one hand, I did not want Mr Darwin to think I was making things up. But, on the other hand, what if it was some new type of lizard? What if I had discovered it? That would surely impress Mr Darwin.

In the end, I decided to remain tight-lipped about what I thought I saw. If I get the chance to explore another island, however, I will definitely keep a look out for swimming lizards.

A surprising find

October 8th, 1835

I am writing this diary entry tonight, sitting at a campfire on dry land. That is correct. On land! We are on another one of the Galápagos Islands, enjoying a wonderful feeling of freedom. I am with Mr Darwin and two others from the *Beagle* – the ship's surgeon and his servant. I cannot believe we will be staying on the island for over a week. I still have to pinch myself to make sure I'm not dreaming. The *Beagle* has gone ahead to search for fresh water and will pick us up upon its return.

Although it has cooled down somewhat tonight, the first thing I noticed as we came ashore today was the heat. It was so hot I could feel the scorching sand through the bottom of my boots. This island is inhabited by unique plants and animals that can somehow survive in these hot, harsh conditions.

I am looking forward to exploring this island more in the coming days. I am also very conscious of impressing Mr Darwin. I feel as if he still takes me for granted, which is frustrating, as I know I've done very adequate work in detailing and documenting his collections.
I very much want Mr Darwin to recognise that I could be his assistant.

October 12th, 1835

Today, Mr Darwin asked me to walk ahead of the group to find a new camp spot. He was travelling to the natural water supply we had found to look for more insect specimens. I would have rather accompanied Mr Darwin, but I held my tongue and did as I was told.

As I scouted about for a good spot to camp, I climbed around a rocky point and startled a lizard lying in the sun. And it startled me! The lizard scurried over the rocks and plunged straight into the ocean. It was under the water for some time, but I watched until I saw it come to the surface. It then pulled itself out of the water and dashed away. I was so excited that I bolted straight back to the others at the main camp. I arrived puffed and sweaty, calling for Mr Darwin.

"He is not here, lad!" the surgeon barked at me. My raucous yelling woke him up and he was most unhappy.

Despite the angry glares I was receiving from both the surgeon and his servant, I told them about the swimming lizard. They both laughed and were full of ridicule. "Lizards do not swim!" they managed to tell me in-between their snickers and their snorts.

Luckily, Mr Darwin was not there to witness my humiliation. I knew then and there that I would not breathe another word of this.

But the annoying thing is I know what I saw. When I get the chance, I will return to that rocky point and find that swimming lizard. I will prove them wrong. Then they will not be laughing.

Proof!

October 16th, 1835

What a day I have had. I am ever so lucky to be sitting here writing about it. It began with a bad idea, although at the time I thought it was a good one.

This morning it occurred to me that we did not have much time left on the island, so I decided I must look for more swimming lizards. It was now or never!

As the sun was rising, I quietly slipped away from the camp. I decided to return to the same spot where I saw the lizard a few days ago. If I was lucky, I would see it again and then I would take Mr Darwin there. If I didn't see the lizard, I would return to camp and the others would be oblivious to my actions. It seemed like an excellent plan.

But, as I trekked across the island, I began to wonder whether it was a good idea after all. The destination was further than I remembered and I started to fear that Mr Darwin and the others would already know I was missing. I put these thoughts out of my mind and continued.

When I finally approached the point and turned the corner, I didn't see a swimming lizard … I saw a whole group of them! Twenty, thirty, maybe even forty. I sucked in one short, sharp breath as I took in the sight. Most of the lizards were lying on the rocks soaking up the sun, but a few were actually in the sea. I found a spot behind a rock and watched in quiet amazement.

It dawned on me that I needed proof that these lizards existed. I took out my notepad and made sketches of what I saw. I also documented the features and behaviours of these unusual creatures.

The large group of lizards basked in the hot sun on rocks. Occasionally they would scamper across the rocks and dive into the water. It was most commonly the biggest of the group that would do this. They are excellent swimmers. They have a flattened tail, which they use to help them move through the rough waves.

They would dive under the water to great depths. I assume they do this to eat. Perhaps they feed on algae that grow deep under the water. There is certainly not a lot of foliage for them to eat on the land. I also observed these creatures eating seaweed off the rocks on the edge of the rocky shore.

I was entranced by what I was witnessing and I lost track of time. It was my empty, hungry stomach that alerted me to how long I'd been away. I needed to get back to the group. Quickly!

I sprung up from my hiding spot and headed swiftly towards camp. As I leapt from rock to rock, my foot suddenly slipped. I stumbled and fell. Thud!

I saw the sea lizards use their strong claws to pull themselves out of the water and back up onto the rocks. After being immersed in the cold seawater, they would then flop onto a rock to warm themselves in the heat of the sun. Like all reptiles, these cold-blooded animals need the sun's warmth to stay alive.

The lizards would occasionally sneeze. It seemed as though their heads were covered in salt. Could it be that the sneezing is a way to rid their bodies of the salt they collect while swimming in the ocean?

When I recovered my breath, I glanced around, trying to figure out what had happened. Soon, I realised that I had fallen down a crevice between three massive volcanic boulders. Apart from a graze down my right forearm I was, unbelievably, unhurt.

After the shock of my fall wore off, I began to panic. I desperately looked around for a way out. I tried to climb up the side of the rock, but it was a sheer face and I kept slipping. Time after time, I slid back down. With each attempt, I was becoming more and more desperate.

It was hopeless. There was no way out.

"Help!" I screamed, hoping against hope that Mr Darwin and the others might be nearby.

I was worried. Very worried. I was alone and afraid. Thoughts raced through my head. Will they ever find me? What if they have to return to the ship? What if the *Beagle* leaves without me?

As the afternoon stretched on, any glimmer of hope I once held steadily slipped away. I squinted through the gap above and could see that the sun was now low in the sky. I was tired. I was hungry. And my situation seemed hopeless. No one knew where I was. How could I have been so stupid?

I drifted in and out of sleep.

Suddenly, I was woken by a noise and was immediately alert and on my feet. I stood still, anxiously listening for a repeat of the noise. Then I heard it again. Footsteps!

"I'm here!" I yelled frantically, with a hoarse voice.

"Syms! Syms!" I heard voices call. And then I saw Mr Darwin, the surgeon and his servant peering down at me. I was overjoyed. I was very glad to see them.

They threw a rope down the deep crevice. I grabbed it and held on for dear life as they pulled me out. I was safe!

"Thank you," I began to say as I looked up at my rescuers. And then I saw their faces.

They were furious!

"What were you thinking, Syms?" said the surgeon, his ruddy face covered in sweat and his mouth set in a hard line. "We did not know where you were. We have spent all day looking for you. You have put us all in danger." The surgeon ranted and raved, and then he and his servant turned on their heels and stormed back in the direction of the camp.

Mr Darwin was angry, too.

"I am sorry, Mr Darwin," I said, in a small voice. I knew then that I had disappointed him and had lost all chance of becoming his assistant.

By then, I had nothing to lose and I told Mr Darwin about seeing the group of swimming lizards. I pleaded for him to come and look for them.

His response took me by surprise. His anger slowly eroded away and he informed me that he had heard about swimming lizards living on these islands. Apparently they're called marine iguanas. And, the best news was that Mr Darwin wanted to see them.

I led Mr Darwin around the point. Wow! The lizards were still there!

"They are quite hideous-looking, aren't they?" Mr Darwin said. But I knew he was impressed.

Back on the Beagle

October 19th, 1835

At times I have felt trapped on this ship, but today I feel differently. After my island adventure, I'm happy and content to be safely on board the *Beagle*.

I built up the courage to show Mr Darwin my notes about the lizards. Mr Darwin read them in silence.
I thought he might have heard my heart beating, I was so nervous. When he slowly started to nod with a satisfied look on his face, I relaxed and smiled to myself.

"This is excellent work, Syms," he finally commented.

And I do not think I misheard him when he said, "You are more like my assistant than a servant. Upon our return to London, you might like to consider working for me, as my assistant."

At this moment, my life was changed forever. Me!
Assistant to Mr Darwin!

And now, as I reflect on the islands around us, I wonder
if people in the future will find them as interesting as
Mr Darwin and I did.

Epilogue

After the voyage of the *HMS Beagle* finished in 1836, Syms Covington continued to work as an assistant to Charles Darwin in London. He helped with preserving and documenting specimens, as well as completing secretarial duties. In 1839, Covington made a decision to settle in Australia. Covington and Darwin had a long-lasting friendship and remained in contact throughout their lives. Covington died in 1861, at the age of 47.

Charles Darwin is one of the world's best-known historical figures. He developed a scientific theory about biological change called *The Origin of Species*, which was published in 1859. Many of his ideas for this theory were first sparked by his observations of the unique and diverse plants and animals he studied on the Galápagos Islands.

Today, the Galápagos Islands archipelago remains a place of wonder. Many people visit it to see the unique animals that live there. It is home to the only ocean-dwelling lizard in the world, the marine iguana. These lizards are endemic to the Galápagos Islands, meaning that they are not found anywhere else in the world.

A note from the author

Many years ago, I read
an information book about
marine iguanas and I was fascinated by these unique
creatures. How unusual for lizards to swim in the ocean!
I have never seen them in the wild, but I imagine that
it would be a great experience. This made me wonder
what it must have been like for people to see these
creatures for the very first time, never even having
heard of their existence.

As I did research for this book, I was captivated by
the story of Charles Darwin and his servant, Syms
Covington, who travelled together on the *HMS Beagle*
in the 1830s. What a different world it was back then!

I wondered what a boy from England would have thought
if he had seen a group of marine iguanas. And so I used
facts from the past about the voyage of the *Beagle* to
write a fictional story, as if it were written in a diary
by Syms Covington.